THE UNKNOWN, GREAT

By the same author:

Wonderment (Zine)
Sometimes I wonder (Zine)
After the Pantomime (Zine)
Computer Hum Lullabies for the Fretful Sleeper (Zine)
A Tender Moment Between Strangers (Girls on Key Press, 2013)
Beatific Toast (Girls on Key Press, 2018)
Clued Up on Current Issues Series (Essential Resources, 2007)
Fabulous Food Series (Essential Resources, 2008)
Thinking Hats Series (Curriculum Concepts, 2005)
Mastering Text—Poetry (User Friendly Resources, 2007)
Ideas Factory Series (Curriculum Concepts, 2007)
Creating Caring Classrooms (User Friendly Resources)
Junior Journal (User Friendly Resources, 2006)

THE UNKNOWN, GREAT

ANNA FORSYTH

RECENT
WORK
PRESS
2015-2025
10 YEARS OF POETRY

The Unknown, Great
Recent Work Press
Canberra, Australia

Copyright © Anna Forsyth, 2025

ISBN: 9781763670143 (paperback)

 A catalogue record for this book is available from the National Library of Australia

All rights reserved. This book is copyright. Except for private study, research, criticism or reviews as permitted under the Copyright Act, no part of this book may be reproduced, stored in a retrieval system, or transmitted in any form by any means without prior written permission. Enquiries should be addressed to the publisher.

Cover image: "'The Woman and the Wolf', Eduardo Luiz" by Pedro Ribeiro Simões, reproduced under Creative Commons Licence 2.0
Cover design: Recent Work Press
Set by Recent Work Press

recentworkpress.com
10 YEARS OF POETRY

Contents

Incidental Music	1
Incremental	2
Longing for Koru	3
Your Absence is a Window	4
The Dress Dummy in the Shower	5
The Mars Ocean Hypothesis	7
Eight Parts Love	8
A Terrain I Recall	10
Grief in the Laundromat	11
Pickled Onions	12
Alex and David	13
Wallpapering	14
Mustering	15
In the Hastings Chill	16
Atlas	17
Possum Skinning/Stink	19
First Impressions of the Inner North	21
Schumann Has Melted My Hands, My Heart	22
Autumn Domain	23
A Contemplative at the Mega Church	24
A Dream of Water	25
A Fragile Kite	26
A Man Walks the Length of Hinemoa Street	27
A People Disappeared	28
A Wake	29
After the Pantomime	30
Alien Skin: a Pantoum	31
Body of Haiku—Insomnia	33
Chai	34
Cove	35
Cracking Up	36
Deflated Santa	37
Four Volcanic Koans	38
Glamping (an A-Z Guide)	41
Hostel Angst	42
In the Interim	43
Little Shoal Bay	44
Lizzy	46
The Diaspora	47
Mist Over Tawharanui	49

Incidental Music

Thrum and syncopation—the blood.
Dad has a muted valve.
Hears a tune in his chest.
One day it will be, The Last Post.

Incidentally, John Cage means feeling
Some-thing, some-thing, near the ribs.
Percussion of it finds nothing untoward
just a subtle set:
Humming lungs,
a feeling no music can describe.

Incremental

I am in the dark habit
of remembering the soft fabric
of your voice, no lyrebird
could mimic, gossamer
so fragile.

At night, I gather blankets
waiting for the dawn of it all
when I become pupa again
emergence, an everyday occurrence
so why do I resist unfolding myself
from your tender spell?

Your voice was oscillating wings
in the dark cavern of my thoughts
I remember the haunting harmonics
those tones, a small grief to me
even then.

Now I know medicine
for reducing dopamine spins
pills for each waveform
if only I could take something
to forget the enveloping
release me from the shadow
of your sonorous presence

For now, I will fool myself
by whispering into your ear
I no longer resonate with you.

Longing for Koru

My face is hidden
behind fern-frond fingers
shoulders the hunched branch
of Pohutukawa

A continuation of koru
in my sister's fernery
reminds me I am nearing the age
of the not possible.
Tui sightings in the flax
outside the hospital
delight, like
the way light plays through a canopy
so, I trudge on
through journals, piles of leaf litter.

In the end the pages are compressed
poems, a felling of something ancient
there's the mulching
and the inevitable bleaching
but there is always a longing
for unfurling adventure
leading me back to forest depths
where poems, like koru
nestle in the deep loam
awaiting the light.

Your Absence is a Window

After Morning Sun *by Edward Hopper*

I remember piecing you together.
Not a morning person, I'd coax you
to the window, where you'd sit
knees firmly clasped.

I let your light play tricks on me
imagining you softer, less angular
painting myself into a corner for you.

All the poems I write now are erasure
shadow boxes, windows, vantages
all opening to a geometry of absence.

This morning's view is from The Hill
edged with metal lace
a perfect metaphor
for how memory
is so cold
but you in morning light
are so etched.

Your absence
that's what this window is
how missing you
I am framed.

The Dress Dummy in the Shower

Don't look down, she says
balanced like a dancer
on duct-taped feet
in some macabre fashion
I am comforted
by the eyelash crawling
like a tear down her cheek.

Did the dummy makeup artist
curl her lip, tempted to name her
to give her a secret
birthmark, scar or mole?

I think of her sisters
marched out in pink plastic
cloned to perfection.

I don't want to look down today.
I stare at the tiles, avoiding
the two small mounds
alien without nipples and
that other inscrutable mound
muzzled and hairless.

My cheeks burn
as the water (my conscience)
scolds me for staring
at her severed arm
my pity mixed with glee.

I watch my reflection
making clumsy dance poses
her breasts refusing
to move in formation.

I want to push her
back into the closet
so, I feel less animal.
Dummy's narrow pelvis tips
in defiance.

I close my eyes there
in that steamy enclosure
I see a million Joanies
(that's her name).

Everything is fixed
they say in unison
through sealed lips.

Dummy,
I whisper to the Joanies
Nothing is fixed.
Dummy.
Dummy.

The Mars Ocean Hypothesis

(Unrequited love)

Asteroids have struck this ocean before.
This was different, it was lava
beneath the canyons melting
all icy materials, becoming
a vast system of subterranean rivers.

Both created tsunamis
those first unthinkable waves.
The first picked up boulders
the size of small houses.
This second wave was obliterating
no-one was there to witness its effect.

I was the Curiosity Rover
thinking myself hospitable
Nasa's *Follow the Water* theme
was always my ethos
but I lacked
a strong Martian magnetosphere
causing sputtering.

The Opportunity Rover
showed it was no longer possible
but evidence of that great flooding
remains.

Eight Parts Love

1.
The poem
in the forest depths
the coil of koru.

2.
Low lighting, the quilt
a thousand dusks.

3.
Capturing fleeting smiles,
silverfish, you
between sheets, pages.

4.
What will it be today?
bitter grapefruit
morning/afternoon.

5.
3am rest stop, he's day glo
lit by cigarette.

6.
Skipping to the end
(Possibly dancing).

7.
In the beginning, words, light
feathers, ancient quills

8.
Divine, our names
in calligraphy
a love scene:
The poem
on a grain of rice
such a seed
(So intricate).

A Terrain I Recall

I can't help but study her
deep fissures in the crags
of her heels, rough terrain.
Have you ever come across
someone whose shape echoes
some forgotten landscape?

The weave of her sandals
cuts across those cliffs
like a badly made fence
cuts across, strange
dusty feet
so hard
for one
so soft
in nature.

Grief in the Laundromat

A portrait

Firstly, it would be a blur of colours
emotive blues, as if through a spin cycle.

Then, a pencil outline of my form
a question mark on cracked leather
(Charcoal detail).

The eyes of course, the focus
blur again to show the ebb and flow.

On the low bench, piles
of sheets, towels
and mismatched socks.

My hair is a tumult, still wet.
My artistic license renders it jet black
for dramatic effect (Indian ink)

A dark woollen coat strewn half-heartedly
covers me (stippled effect).

The hands seem out of place
White knuckled and firmly pressed
together, as if in prayer.

Pickled Onions

For Dad

Love is industrious, even though
    homemade risotto is bland
needs tomato sauce, or something…

Sorry.

Two household chefs live in me
    Mum burritos-again or gourmet toast
then you:
    resourceful and meticulous
menus for little appreciation.

Your homemade beer   e x p l o d e d
    so I heard
as bottled-up things tend to.
    Timing never right.…

But I won't let things ferment
    conversations have a *mise en place* now
like your terrible fridge-scraps stew.
Now, consider the more bitter memories
    a thing of the past.

Alex and David

For Alex, Tuesday night became a long, winding tunnel. The podcast, Attenborough in Paradise, had her thinking. Quest for something or other. All we need to do is…down goes the counterweight. Now I'm leaving the dark world of the forest. Alex was still in the dark forest. She was on a trail that was travelling through one in slow motion. She had time to capture still frames in her mind. What first drew me to the bear? One bear really caught my interest. I met her when she was just a cub, thirteen years ago. It's great to see her after all this time, but does she remember me? I certainly remember her. Alex was tossing and turning, in between yawns. She stretched her body out under the feather duvet. David's voice: A raffishly handsome insect with long, elegant legs and a glossy black and scarlet body. The sound of rain. Sleep evaded her.

By morning, Alex was exhausted. Exhausted. David is from another planet. Does he even sleep? Does he hug orangutans in his dreams, in Borneo…no wait…Sumatra? The room is a stage set. Just a nondescript chair and table as props. A poster of an orangutan on the wall. Save the orangutans. Enter stage left. Alex is enjoying her Marmite jaffle when she hears David's key in the door. Badly written script. David addresses the audience: In all my years of exploration, these are the creatures I find most curious.

Wallpapering

In those ads
The happy couple always wear overalls
they are always painting a wall white.
It is customary to kiss while wallpapering
and to surprise your lover
by playfully lunging at them with the roller.
You too can have great interest
rates, or insure yourself for a premium.
You too can have the luxury of
recreational house painting
and playful paint roller fights.
What more could you ask for?

Mustering

Cissy is not afraid, although
it's a dusty, nomadic job, up there
at Top End
it is the unforgiving territory.
As a child, she dreamed
about the wild west.
Bill's first draft was Brunette Downs
sleeping with Cissy in a swag.
Later, they called him:
Pearl of the North.
After reading the story
I go to buy grits, or a steak.
What about that unexplored territory?
I take in the long view on the bridge
up and around the corner.
I will forgive wildly.
I am the helicopter mustering pilot.

In the Hastings Chill

I was locked out of the wharenui
wrapped in a sleeping bag to stare
at Maui's silhouette on the prow of te waka
the moon creates an aura around him
two tricksters who know how to spin a yarn
one, the size of his fish (the north island)
the other the warrior queen of shadow play
and every ghost story.
I am shivering in the Hastings chill
Maui only knows biceps and importance
watched eternally by tupuna, the muscled pose.
I want to see his shadow
side, soft underbelly
but the moon pulls the strings
sucks me in to that dark story again
and I shiver.

It's broad daylight, but
I saw you hovering near the harbour
like a new astrological sign
a trick of the light
you said you were with me
now I believe you
transfiguring my loneliness
with your untameable belief
in me.

Atlas

1.
She who holds the world
on her shoulders
mother Atlas, by alias
to uphold, support
enduring Atlas
the celestial axis
on which all children
revolve.

2.
Atlas as the mountain range
Divine Feminine
only lofty to the weary
it's lonely at the top
waiting for the one
the pilgrim
willing to suffer altitude sickness
to break the spell.

3.
Feminism is the original
astronomer
Atlas extending her reach
creating lenses
mapping the heavens
capturing the infinite
possibilities

4.
The geography evolves
women wait
for the new cartographers
the brave retellers
of her-story
their bodies
futures
on the line.

Possum Skinning/Stink

He skins stoats and possums
keeping them intact if possible
still bloody.
The fresher the better.

He sits on the side of the road
cross-legged with his knife
cuts with precision, across
the back of the creature.
One slip might ruin a good pelt.

I remember him in his suit.
The road took a turn, screeches
the brakes, he couldn't resist.
So perfect!

My brother would be pleased.
He wears a Davy Crocket hat.
Runs around, possum tail swishing.

The knife was wet.
He hit the musk gland.
No hope for the suit.
The pelt, the skin, bummer.
Such a good one.

What a beauty!
Not a drop of blood, but
a ton of musk.
Mum put an end to possum skinning
after that
after all what does one do

with a freezer full of stinky stoats
and a stinky husband?

First Impressions of the Inner North

The first thing you notice is her scent
she dabs each corner
with that coffee you like

It's not that she plays hard to get exactly
but she's not a cold, concrete bitch
like Auckland.

On Westgarth bridge
I light a cigarette
check her out when no one's looking

I'm intrigued by her poise
like a woman on the verge.

Schumann Has Melted My Hands, My Heart

Only Caroline and I
feel sick
during Feldenkrais

Professor Graham
watches over her protégé:
I don't have the special awareness.

Elsa's hands dance
through the Brahms
Te Quero
corrects us on our vowels
at the Tiatro Colón:
lo ro ro ro.

I don't have the spatial awareness.
Schumann has melted my hands,
my heart.

Autumn Domain

We are idling carefully
through broken leaves, bark
stalling the wind's bite
in a shared coat, laughing.

Giggling at trees
we will quiet the rustle
of yellow rain
jackets aside, held in arms.

We are not waiting for skies to break
or watching wide eyed
for the end, snapping
to fend for ourselves.

We are foraging together
despite the cutty grass
planting secret trees
the fruit of our safe keeping.

A Contemplative at the Mega Church

Neon cross outside
the interior is beige

a figure turns
ankles inward
thoughts tucked
in jean pockets
folded prayers.

Visions of solitude
Christ withdrawing
into the garden.

Clapping punctures
the air, my soft heart.

A Dream of Water

When I crease my pillow
a dream of water persists
crystalline sea to be precise.
Being under a water sign
the urge to swim
is like an ache

A Fragile Kite

Mother Theresa
didn't believe in God
towards the end
they say
I'm not surprised
I wouldn't either
living in the slums of Calcutta
among the leprous
and diseased
drowning in their own despair
In Auckland
far from those cesspits
they say the harbour bridge
is susceptible to high winds
I am a child
standing by the edge and leaning
precariously
clutching this fragile kite
called belief

A Man Walks the Length of Hinemoa Street

For my grandfather, Hector, a prisoner of war

I spot him on the corner
outside Hill Methodist.
(Neon cross, beige interior).
I think of what was carried
on other hills, bush tracks
on other backs, splintered.
He was an engineer
He was a…

In the midday sun, he limps
toward the waterfront, I see him
off the bus and squinting
clutching a hard blue suitcase.
His face is tanned leather.
His eyes, once mischievous
now humorless.

I see him cross the road
avoiding Chinese takeaways.

I follow my grandfather, shirted
ghost with jutting ribs,
past the plump café goers.

At the traffic lights he turns,
shows his prized possession:
his suitcase;
a wealth of cigarette butts.

A People Disappeared

I do not see them
displayed in restaurant fronts
on Gertrude Street
posed with partners and chardonnays
I do not see them with jutting chins
 polished reflections of each other
on Collins
looking up, then down up, then down
I do not see them

Sometimes a man will call out to me
on the corner of Smith and Langridge
I'm not sure if he's a ghost
but he walks
as if he has already disappeared

A Wake

As we make our way
from shore to shore
the sunlight makes white ghost fish
translucent
just below the surface
of our trailing wake.
Wake.
The word brings to mind
a family, gathering
after a funeral
small pastries in hand,
the tears ebbing and flowing.
I imagine the loved one
sailing off into the distance.
Not asleep
but awake
and waving

After the Pantomime

We will laugh
at the transparency of our masks
the pain of wearing them forgotten
as we dance open-faced and naked.

I imagine we will marvel
at the true audience of our chaos.

You will quip about Shakespeare
and I will insist
that I never acted a day
in my life.

Alien Skin: a Pantoum

I cannot see the solar system up close

All the stars look the same—a repetition

The skin on my wrists is semi-translucent

Tonight, I have a shimmering meniscus

All stars look the same—a repetition

Contemplating this alien skin

I wonder if Angelina Jolie ever fails to recognise herself?

What would I look like without skin?

Contemplating this alien skin

Looking at objects for too long makes them appear alien

Staring at a word blurs its meaning

Do I truly know what it means to feel alien?

Looking at objects too much makes them appear alien.

When did *you* become *other*?

There's a story about humans being sculpted from clay

What are aliens made of?

When did *you* become *other*?

I've often felt a sense of *otherness* here

My people imposed on you and I'm sorry

Thank-you for keeping your mana.

I've often felt a sense of *otherness* here

My mother taught me I am not of this world

But we are all made of the same stuff

We all have clay feet and I'm sorry

My mother taught me I am not of this world

I always stared into space as a child

I think I will stop contemplating aliens tonight

And put this alien skin to bed

Body of Haiku—Insomnia

I watch the shadows; darting ghosts and seeds of light / the moon's eye is open
My scorched throat is dry; I listen to breath's whistle / the birds are rising
Hands sleep—not for long, now they gather up blankets / dream of a grim reaper
My heartbeat trembling, mountains quaking on my chest / nipples—frozen flags.
Vivaldi's Seasons, this will be my lullaby / all four concertos

Chai

I sip slowly on warm chai
The day before, my blood had gone cold
Diagnosis?
Spiritual anemia
My soul leeched of its iron
But between then and now
I have remembered
I have chosen chai
I drink deep of the antidote
Warm life
seeps through the protective fabric
around my heart muscle
As I sit entwined
In a lover's knot
Feel the unbroken protection of arms
I can see the reaper's shadow
Out of the corner of my eye
But it brings no terror
Because I know that valleys have ends
And I cannot forget
The shepherd's crook

Cove

Your hand along the coastline
my lower back recalls, sudden
high tide swells at Tawharanui
soft feet tracing the shore's outline
please send me this smooth reminder.

The sound of your skin
your groan, soft eddies
desire you create in me.

A sarong billows from driftwood
in my dream, can we lay twined
let the warm sun dapple us

find the cove again
my back
take me there
take me back
to Tawharanui.

Cracking Up

Sometimes existence
is mere air, mere breath
fewer blue and pink balloons
fewer bright thoughts
tied with string
more the nightmare
costume party

so many iterations
of ghastly fabrics

a never-ending parade
of all my hair mistakes

precious time spent
with pretenders
make up
for all the cracking
up.

Deflated Santa

Like you,
I have been through many skins, a cicada
sings and I understand
what it is to be like the onion
but I only cry when you do.
I cherish the unintended doodle
calligraphy.
It's that or the dustbin.

There have been many
new-pen promises.
I've protected your dreams
on those dark-ink nights.
I won't tell who is full of hot air
and who is the deflated Santa.

Your secrets are safe with me.

Four Volcanic Koans

1. Maungawhau

It is the highest point of the city.

As a worship leader
I was responsible
for taking people
to the high places
I did so dutifully
smiling at horizon lights
until my cheeks ached.

Nobody told me the apex
would also be hollow
desire always
latent, aching.

I didn't take the van loads
of Christian tourists into account
their cameras always at the ready.

They expected the flow
of the Holy Spirit
at all times.

For me
the underground
water reservoir
was something private;
something reverent;
nature best observed
in silence.

When is a volcano
not a volcano?

2. Rangitoto Island

Children can disrupt the view
depending on your vantage
on Takapuna beach
Rangitoto's shape looms
so I lie flat on my sarong

for now…

A volcano, her lava
flow is unseen.
What do I exist for?

3. Mt Roskill (Puketapapa)

The area around it
was called the Bible belt.
I've known a few of those.
It took time to stop
beating *myself* up.

Like Puketapapa
I've been excavated
forgiveness flows
like the water here.

My heart container
made by fire fountains.

What burns, yet heals?

4. Auckland Domain (Pukekawa)

The Maori called it
The Hill of Bitter Memories.
Now host to war memorials.

I can stretch out here
the domain of memories
sunlight branching into each room
shedding light on each small victory.

One farmer plants
a sweet seed;
the other bitter.
Are they both still seeds?

Glamping (an A-Z Guide)

All Modes here
Bunny burrows
Camp motha, climbing mountains, cold as!
Drunken campervanners, dandelion roots on dunes
Everyone pitches in
Finn jokes, farts, fuel gifts, frisbee fails, flax bush washing line
Gumboots christened, galloping glampers, gannets run on solar power, gorse prick
Happy campers, heaters made from terracotta
Inventions made from cans
Jeff the redhead planting barefoot
Kerry asks 'get his number?'
Ladybug apples, lost sock
Marshmallows, mud-caked gumboots, manuka
No sleep, niggly sniff
OJ - freshly squeezed
Pukeko friends, Planting - Pohutakawa, pancaking
Quick - get out of the rain
Rain, rain go away! Road trippin', rizomes
Sunshine prayers answered, slug visitors, sausage sizzling, sneaky ciggies
Tawharanui! Tent pegs, torchlit toilet trips, takahi coming!
Under the stars
Vast hills, vacillating weather
Winter ocean swims, Wetland wading, wine in plastic cup
Xtreme digging
Yellow light
Zzzzzzzzz

Hostel Angst

Thoughts turn my core
into a precipice
on my bed, I yearn
for gravity, touch
the bunk's steel
with my feet, to keep
from falling.

In the Interim

In the space between
See ya round
and *Hello again…*

millions of birds
gather whatever it is they gather
to make their sodden nests.

I don't blink that often
but I'm sure I've done it a fair bit
although not for flirting
that's only when you're here.

Lots of water evaporates
(not tears, don't get me wrong)
windows fog, then clear.
I sleep
(sometimes fretfully, sometimes not)
A clock ticks solemnly.

Little Shoal Bay

It was a favourite spot for years
you couldn't keep me out of the water
down there
I was always a water baby
as a child
The beach itself is not that nice
it's always muddy and slippery
underfoot
with little pin prick worm holes
and cutty mussel shells
I don't really know how they stick there
like that
There's too many rocks
and a long thread
of dirty cream foam
peppered with leaf skeletons
and lots of flotsam
bits
and pieces
of dead birds
that made me jump
when I saw
their matted feathers
and cold eyes staring up
glassy
black beads
I was such a timid child
I never ventured very far
around the rocks
not like mum
she was always hunting
for washed up treasures

an old glass bottle
or half a spiral shell
to add to her windowsill collection
of odds and sods

Lizzy

She is pitch perfect
light on her feet
sings, an anthem
I don't know
but wish I did.

The horse jumps
off the page
at her command.

The Diaspora

We are spreading
Marmite on the table edge
Like when I was a child.
We are spreading
Ivy legs clinging
To buildings reassembled.

Send our birds from the bush
But keep them in hand
Speed dial to London, New York
Melbourne.

Flight paths endlessly redrawn
Painted arrows quiver
From the middle of nowhere
Sent to target
For supplies
Or Kmart
They are the same wherever you go.

Bring back a jar of marmite
Old habits die hard
We are spreading ourselves
Promiscuous, thin
slices of vogels.

Meanwhile, the travel bug spreads
Sickening at airports
Are you eating properly?
Back at the bush track near Tawharanui
We are pushing out fence posts.
How far out

Can the boundary lines reach?
How far can the umbilical cord stretch
Before breaking completely?

What about reverse migration?
Flip the record, play it backwards
So it is always summer at Tawharanui
Van Morrison
Warm love through heat waves
And cold changes
Always with a marmite sandwich.

Mist Over Tawharanui

To every misty-eyed sailor
every seabird searching
for the next updraught
Let your tears flow
like lace seaweed
she says
let me buoy you
til the clear sky
resurrection
til your seabird soul
is birthed
to the horizon, waiting
beyond the shadow
of night's small death.

Notes

pg 32 'Mana'—strength of pride and spirit in Maori

Acknowledgements

I am deeply grateful to all the editors of the following publications, in which these poems are published:

'The Dress Dummy in the Shower', *Baby Teeth Online Journal* (2018)
'Eight Parts Love', *Not Very Quiet* (2018)
'A Terrain, I recall', *Not Very Quiet* (2019)
'Alex and David', *Bonsai,* CUP, (2018)
'Atlas', *The Alphabet of Women*, Ginninderra Press (2022)

About the Author

Anna Forsyth is an editor, poet, and event producer originally from New Zealand. In 2014, she founded Girls on Key, a feminist poetry organisation, which has hosted regular poetry readings for women and gender diverse poets in Sydney, Wollongong, Castlemaine, Melbourne, Newcastle, and Auckland. Her poems and short stories have appeared in numerous journals in print and online including *Headland, FourW, Poetry New Zealand, Landfall, NScribe, Not Very Quiet, Baby Teeth* and *Sidestream* among others. She was the joint winner of the NAIDOC Red Room poetry prize 2018 and the Unity Books Short Story Competition, 2017 (NZ). She is the publishing manager and editor of Girls on Key Press, focusing on female and gender diverse poets. She currently lives in Auckland, New Zealand.

www.ingramcontent.com/pod-product-compliance
Lightning Source LLC
Chambersburg PA
CBHW030535080526
44585CB00014B/961